YOUR KNOWLEDGE HAS VALUE

- We will publish your bachelor's and master's thesis, essays and papers

- Your own eBook and book - sold worldwide in all relevant shops

- Earn money with each sale

Upload your text at www.GRIN.com and publish for free

Bibliographic information published by the German National Library:

The German National Library lists this publication in the National Bibliography; detailed bibliographic data are available on the Internet at http://dnb.dnb.de .

This book is copyright material and must not be copied, reproduced, transferred, distributed, leased, licensed or publicly performed or used in any way except as specifically permitted in writing by the publishers, as allowed under the terms and conditions under which it was purchased or as strictly permitted by applicable copyright law. Any unauthorized distribution or use of this text may be a direct infringement of the author s and publisher s rights and those responsible may be liable in law accordingly.

Imprint:

Copyright © 2018 GRIN Verlag
Print and binding: Books on Demand GmbH, Norderstedt Germany
ISBN: 9783668701533

This book at GRIN:

https://www.grin.com/document/424903

D.M.C. Wayne

The Future of Education. Advantages and Disadvantages of Online Education

GRIN Verlag

GRIN - Your knowledge has value

Since its foundation in 1998, GRIN has specialized in publishing academic texts by students, college teachers and other academics as e-book and printed book. The website www.grin.com is an ideal platform for presenting term papers, final papers, scientific essays, dissertations and specialist books.

Visit us on the internet:

http://www.grin.com/

http://www.facebook.com/grincom

http://www.twitter.com/grin_com

Table of Content

Introduction 2
Characteristics of Future Education 2
Online Education 5
Advantages of Online Education 5
Disadvantages of Online Education 6
Recommendation and Conclusion 8
References 9

Introduction

Over the past several decades the rapid technological advancement has had an impact on every aspect of human life and education has been one of the most important beneficiaries of this phenomenon. However as technology continues to take a central role in today's society, educational experts and professionals have raised concerns on the possible impacts that this will have not just on the system but also on the students and the society as whole. With some critics arguing that technology would in the future replace human intelligence (Damary, Markova & Pryadilina, 2017). This, they argue would be as a result of the assumption of control by technologies over a considerable measure of undertakings and capacities that educators have been educating their students in the conventional education system. It is the position of this paper that despite the rise of technology and the central role it is now playing in the society, Education faces no threat, rather with the changing world; technology will only be driving force behind the restructuring of the education model education as it aligns itself to the global changes.

Characteristics of Future Education

Conventional learning methods continue to develop with the aid of the increased innovation and advances in the technological front. Individuals will have access to better learning resources whenever they require, this has immense academic importance to education (Wong, 2017). Individuals all around the globe will be able to access enhanced portability because of the flexibility and potential that online learning gives. Additionally, as more institutions continue to adopt these online platforms as part of their core education process, formal scholastic online learning instruction is becoming legitimately accepted as part of the mainstream educational frameworks. Some of the features of future education include

- **Personalized learning**: Each student will have the opportunity to learn with educational instruments that adjust to their abilities to perform or complete a given task. This implies that students who are considered to be above average in terms of knowledge is concerned, will have the chance to be tested with appropriately challenging assignments and tasks when a specific level is accomplished (Wong, 2017). Students who encounter troubles with a subject will get the chance to hone more until the point when they have fully grasped the required concepts at each stage. As such, students will be emphatically strengthened over the course of their learning process. This can bring about to positive learning encounters and will reduce the measure of students losing self-confidence on their own individual educational and scholarly capacities. Besides, through such an environment, instructors will have the capacity to unmistakably identify the students who may require help in specific areas of their studies. Consequently, it would be easy to put in place the measures to ensure that they have the required assistance in overcoming those challenges.

- **Project based**: As professions continuously adapt to the current shift towards a future independent and global economy, it is essential for students to adjust and adapt to a more project centered institutional and working environments. This implies that students must have the ability to effectively the knowledge they have learned in relatively short periods of time to an assortment of real life circumstances. Online education offers hierarchical, community oriented, and time administration aptitudes can be instructed as essentials that each student will find to be of immense use in their professions and careers later in life.

- **Diverse Place and Time:** in future students will be afforded the chance to attend and be part of their respective classes at diverse times and in different geographical areas. Through E-Learning apparatuses, remote and self-paced classes will be a common feature. As such, the arrangement made for classes will depend on the content and objectives of study (Sydorenko & Fris, 2016). This means that the theoretical part of the learning process will be done outside the conventional classroom setting and facilitated through virtual based connection/ o the other hand, the practical part of the coursework will be taught in the traditional face to face classroom setting.

- **Free choice**: In spite of the fact that each subject taught at educational institutions, the means to attaining those objective for each individual student vary significantly. Correspondingly to the personalized learning background, students will have the capacity to adjust their learning process with devices and techniques that they feel are essential to them. Students will also have access to a varied range of educational gadgets and framework apparatus, distinctive projects and procedures as it relates to their individual learning and educational inclinations. BYOD (Bring Your Own Device), Flipped classrooms and blended learning are some of the vital terminologies and key words that characterize this change (Sydorenko & Fris, 2016).

- **Field Experience**: Since technology and innovation can encourage more productivity in specific areas, educational modules will prepare for abilities that exclusively require human learning and physical interaction. In this way, involvement in 'the field' will be underscored inside all of the courses. Schools will give more chances to understudies to get genuine aptitudes that are illustrative to their employments (Ally & Prieto-Blázquez, 2014). As such, this implies that the existent educational programs will make more space for all students to satisfy obligatory internship programs, tutoring undertakings and cooperation ventures within their areas of specialty.

- **Data Analysis and Interpretation**: In spite of the fact that science is viewed as one of three most significant literacies, it is unmistakably identifiable that the manual aspect of this crucial literacy is continuously being watered down and may become irrelevant in the future. Technology and new innovations on this end are rapidly taking up the statistical analysis exercises will soon deal with each measurable examination, through describing and breaking down information to project future patterns and occurrences. In this manner, the human elucidation of this information will turn into a considerably more critical feature of future educational curriculums (Ally & Prieto-Blázquez, 2014). Applying the hypothetical information to numbers, and utilizing human thinking to induce rationale and patterns from these information will turn into a key new part of this proficiency.
- **Change in Student Assessment methods**: since the courseware platforms will be used in the evaluation of students at each level of education, the use of Q&A in such scenario will become irrelevant. Numerous experts and professional sin the education sector, including other external stakeholders have argued that the current use of Q&A has been designed in way that students are able to cram course materials for the purpose of passing an exam, only to forget all about it afterwards (Ally & Prieto-Blázquez, 2014). Teachers stress that exams may not truly quantify what students ought to be equipped for when they enter their first occupation. As the genuine academic capacities of a student can be estimated amid their learning experience, the utilization of their insight is best tried through real life applications of theoretical knowledge in the field.
- **Curricula Ownership by the Student**: As education progresses in to the future, the critical role and involvement of students in the development of their curricula will be fundamentally increased. The ability to maintain efficient and effective educational modules that is contemporary, forward and helpful can only be attained when the inputs of seasoned educational experts and youngsters are considered and used in its development. The essential contribution from students on the substance and sturdiness of these courses will be an unquestionable requirement for a comprehensive study program.
- **The Role of Mentoring will be Key**: In the future, the relation between a student and the school will have incorporated a great amount of freedom in to the learning experience, to an extent that mentoring will become a key factor in determining an individual academic success As such, the role of educators and instructors in all academic institutions will continue to act as crucial central points in a world of extensive information the students will be in. Despite the fact that the eventual fate of education

may appear to be remote at this moment in time, the role of educational institutions and teachers are essential and indispensable to scholastic execution and continuity.

Online Education

Learning has and continues to be a key aspect of human life. From a conventional point of view learning and education has been connected and restricted to a classroom setting, a phenomenon that has been challenged by the rise of technology (Damary, Markova & Pryadilina, 2017). Through technological advances the concept of online classes has become common as more and more educational institutions become increasingly committed to adopting this learning framework. The online environment is changing continuously and it represents a great opportunity for individuals to access education in a way that was never known to be possible before. This includes the access of quality education by individuals in areas where the standards of education may be low. Through online classes individuals are able to find and enroll in programs that suit and are in alignment with their unique and personal preference and capacities. The value and inclination to online learning in future will be significantly high and will have an impact on the quality and access to education.

It is evaluated that e-learning is utilized by estimated 100 million individuals' globally. According to researchers, the rise of E-learning will experience a continuous growth and development. Global experience recommends that, given astounding instructive substance and equipped course plan, the viability of e-learning cannot be argued as being sub-par in comparison to the conventionally adopted classroom or face to face system between the student and the educator. In order to fully recognize and understand the impact of such a move from the conventional classroom learning experience to a virtual online system it is imperative to identify the advantages and disadvantages of this significant and requisite framework adoption.

Advantages of Online Education

- **Flexibility**: I distance and online learning, students have the opportunity to participate and complete their coursework and studies from anyplace in the world, through the internet. This enables the students to work whenever it is appropriate without squeezing in planned classes to an already bustling life (Arkorful & Abaidoo, 2015).
- **Improves Communication**: By integrating technology into the process of teaching, the level communication and connection between the students and their educators is significantly improved. For instance; the teacher can use power points and pictures to further advance the understanding of students on a particular concept.

- **Improved Access to Education**: technology in future will be a key a part of most human activities and education will not be an exception. The access to technology has penetrated to the remote areas of developing nations where access to physical teaching and education materials might be a challenge. Therefore, through online learning, individuals in these areas will have access to a huge and extensive access to diverse educational materials such as, books and articles, some for free.
- **Ease in access of materials**: through technology an instructors is able to access a huge catalog of data, information and material that is relevant to their field of specialty quickly and on demand (Arkorful & Abaidoo, 2015). For instance through touch screen boards the teacher can retrieve and access specific data and thus augmenting the pace of the lessons being taught.
- **Accommodation of a broader and larger student base**: Through online classes students are able to interact with individuals from diverse backgrounds and culture. Consequently, this aids the students in understanding diverse approaches to a similar challenge which enriches the learning process.

Disadvantages of Online Education

- **There is a need for a great deal of self-discipline**: In the conventional type of education system, there's typically an arrangement of rules and regulations that all students are expected to adhere strictly adhere to. This is a pivotal perspective as it gives the students an obligation and purpose in their academic life. Consequently, it ensures that the students follow the instructions and tasks given to them by their teachers and educators. With regards to online education the standard significantly differs since in this education framework, the student has been given a great deal of freedom and thus affecting the ability of the educator to have a direct control of what the student is doing. If not well managed, this kind of freedom can irreparably damage the focus of the student as far as academics are concerned. Online courses accompany strict due dates as it relates to handing in of assignments and such tasks as given by the educator. In the event that a student is not able to effectively manage the time allocated for the completion of the assignment the potential of failure is significantly augmented. Consequently, online education gives the student complete freedom by taking the assumption that each individual student is be self-discipline enough in ensuring that tasks and assignments are completed or in attendance of scheduled online classes so as to ensure success.
- **Isolation**: Isolation is a major concern that has been fronted by various educational experts on the rise and adoption of online education. The significance of the interaction

between students and the r fellow colleagues in the achievement of both academic and personal goals cannot be overstated. It is through interaction with fellow students that an individual is able identify the areas of study that they would like to pursue (Thorpe, 2002). Additionally, it is from such interactions, that the fire of academic rivalry will emanate and illuminate within a student, rousing them to work harder in order to make a decent name for themselves in their areas of study. The ability to interact and collaborate with fellow students also ensures that an individual is able to build and maintain a professional network of individuals who might be of help in later careers. Thusly, when an individual settles for online courses, it implies that they will have to rely on their personal analysis and understanding skills since there is no other individual with them to brainstorm with. In the event that they are in connection with another individual on the same online course, it means spending more time on the internet which also gets tiresome and uninteresting.

- **Inability to Directly Interact with the Educator**: There has been a contention that online instruction makes a monolog rather than discourse type of learning experience. This is a fundamental concern in light of the fact that the significance of direct association between the student and heir educator cannot be overstated. In the conventional classroom setting, the instructor is able to directly and instantaneously screen a student's non-verbal communication so as to guarantee that they are focused on what is being taught to them; the teacher can decipher when the student appears to be distracted by something, when they haven't understood a concept or, even in case where the student may not be interested in a particular subject (Thorpe, 2002). As such they are able to take the necessary corrective measures to ensure that the student is able to bring back their minds and concentrate on what they are teaching. However, when it comes to online education, none of these verbal cues can be conceived by the educator and as such the possibility of the student to understand is lowered. In addition, conventional type classes, unlike online classes, allow the teacher to effectively apply measures that can augment the interest of the students on a particular topic through their physical interactions and explanations. The use of online education, scarcely offers such an opportunity to the educator and thus has become one of the major disadvantages of online learning

Recommendation and Conclusion

Technological advancements have been a central feature of the 20th century and continue to be a key influence in most aspects of human life including education. As technology continues to take a central role in today's society, education professionals and experts have raised concerns on the possible impacts that this will have not just on the system but also on the students and the society as whole. Some of the critics against the shift from conventional education methods have argued that that technology would in the future replace human intelligence.

The most considerable argument that raises concern on the ascent of online learning is the nature of online courses in contrast with regular courses as it relates to the equality of education that the students will receive. In this context most individuals are raising issues on whether such online courses are sufficient for employers and to take note and consider their effectiveness. The second greatest contention is the present reality that is faced by numerous individuals from low income backgrounds; in spite of the upgrades made in this area over the past few years, it is a reality that individuals from these underprivileged areas do not have the level of fundamental access expected to profit from online internet learning. It is, in this regard, essential to note that various global statistics and experience has shown that given appropriate instructive substance and equipped course plan, the viability of e-learning cannot be argued as being sub-par in comparison to the conventionally adopted classroom or face to face system between the student and the educator. According to critics there are various affirmation signs that point at the inability of individuals from poor backgrounds to access the benefits that can be available to them on these platforms, as fronted by online learning organizations and promoters. There are various organizations and institutions that are endeavoring to grow people's access to higher education through both legal and academic means. Due to this increased interest on the subject, it is quite plausible to argue, with relative certainty that this would be realized within the next few decades or maybe less. Regardless of the rise of technology, and the key role it will play in the education sector, it will only be the driving force behind the restructuring of the education model education as it aligns itself to the global changes.

References

Ally, M., & Prieto-Blázquez, J. (2014). What is the future of mobile learning in education?. *International Journal of Educational Technology in Higher Education*, *11*(1), 142-151

Arkorful, V., & Abaidoo, N. (2015). The role of e-learning, advantages and disadvantages of its adoption in higher education. *International Journal of Instructional Technology and Distance Learning*, *12*(1), 29-42.

Damary, R., Markova, T., & Pryadilina, N. (2017). Key Challenges of On-Line Education in Multi- Cultural Context. *Procedia-Social and Behavioral Sciences*, *237*, 83-89

Sydorenko, N., & Fris, I. (2016). Self-Regulation of Behavior and Its Features in Future Teachers. *Science and Education*, (5), 246-251.

Thorpe, M. (2002). Rethinking learner support: The challenge of collaborative online learning. *Open learning*, *17*(2), 105-119

Wong, T. (2017). The future of education. *Independence*, *42*(1), 4

YOUR KNOWLEDGE HAS VALUE

- We will publish your bachelor's and master's thesis, essays and papers

- Your own eBook and book - sold worldwide in all relevant shops

- Earn money with each sale

Upload your text at www.GRIN.com and publish for free